Etiquette
of an Intern

Workbook & Journal

HOW TO APPROACH SECURING
YOUR DREAM INTERNSHIP

KATE STAGG

First published in Australia 2018
by Karen Mcdermott

www.karenmcdermott.com.au

National Library of Australia Cataloging-in-Publisher data:

ISBN 978-0-6481466-0-5
eBook ISBN 978-0-6481906-0-8

Designer: Parklife Group Pty Ltd™

www.parklifegroup.com.au

SPECIAL THANKS TO:

MY PARENTS, DAVE & PAULINE
What an amazing unbringing you gave me, full of unconditional love, support and drive, which led to me to believe anything is possible.

KAREN McDERMOTT
You helped me find my inspiration. I am forever thankful.

ERICA ORMSBY
Thank you for your contribution to this book and for your enthusiatic approach to our industry and its educational future.

DONNA BATES
For giving me encouragement, with whatever I am thinking, to think bigger!

CARTE BLANCHE GREETINGS
Stephen Haines, Carole Kavanagh, Helen Phillippe, Art & Repro Department.

Etiquette of an Intern

Written by Kate Stagg, CEO | Parklife Group Pty Ltd™

ParklifeGroup™
Digital | Graphics | Print | Products

Foreword

By Erica Ormsby

Coordinator for Design
at Murdoch University

Education can provide the essential tools of trade for up and coming professionals. Theoretical perspectives alongside practical methods can facilitate students in understanding their craft. Education however can be limiting. We can work away to our hearts content knowing that our methodology and historical understanding of our field are powerful for our employment. However, this is only half of the job. Communicating effectively with clients and successfully working alongside other people can be extraordinarily challenging. Most professions involve ongoing interactions with multiple disciplines and the majority of workplaces require the development of successful human relationships in order to do the job at hand. Internships are a beneficial tool, that allow up and coming professionals to grasp the broader workings of employment beyond the practical methods. They may act as a baptism by fire but internships allow graduating students to test the waters of real life work environments and get a taste of what might be expected of them within their profession.

Embarking on the journey to employment after many years in education can seem overwhelming. It can feel like it is impossible to prepare for the unknown.

Internships can expose unexpected challenges that are not apparent from learning in a classroom. Clients are not always easy to get along with and deadlines can be stressful. On top of this, collaboration is a necessity for most modern professionals. Whether it be collaborating with other people in your field or working with other disciplines, the future of employment lies in interacting with many people to get the job done. Internships provide a chance for up and coming professionals to gain an understanding of the in and outs of working among their local or international industries.

As a designer for over seventeen years and an educator for over thirteen years, the most important thing that I have been able to teach my students, is that everyone is human; clients, employers and employees. I have been able to share my own professional stories of successful and not so successful client relationships and most importantly, what I have learnt from them. I know now that most people want to develop successful working relationships. Employers want new staff to fit into their workplace, employees want to fit into their new workplace and clients want to be assured that they have hired the right professional for their job. Internships are an effective way to test a potential working relationship for all parties involved.

This book acts as a valuable support guide to securing an internship. It reveals what to expect when entering a professional space for the first time and provides advice on how to navigate the unknown environments of employment.

Most importantly, this book promotes up and coming professionals to source the place of work that is the right fit for them. It inspires the readers of this book to take a moment and consider what really drives them; what do they really want from their profession before they choose a place of employment. No two jobs are the same, no two clients are the same, no two people are the same. This book is an essential resource for not only establishing an internship but also for finding out if a place of employment is the perfect fit.

Erica Ormsby

Introduction

"Anything is possible if
you've got enough nerve."

– J.K.Rowling

The book you are holding was inspired by a desire to encourage youth to be driven and motivated in their quest for career success. It is designed to act as a support tool, to help guide and nurture an intern through the daunting journey of entering the workforce.

My journey started when I was a shy creative teenager, desperate to break into the world of animation. Understanding my small hometown of Bognor Regis had limited resources when it came to nurturing my 'Pixar' dream, I turned to a local advertising design agency to offer me my first glimpse of a design studio. Unlike some of my sixteen-year-old friends, I wasn't willing to waste my internship tidying a cupboard in an accountancy firm, just to miss out on classroom attendance. Looking back now, I realise I had a type of personality that although shy, was determined and driven. I didn't once undertake the help of my parents in securing my internship, other than to drive me to deliver the resumes that I had painstakingly prepared, with my rough knowledge of Word. It wasn't a matter of my parents not wanting to help, they had just instilled in us that if we wanted something, we were to go get it!

"If you don't ask, you don't get." - Stevie Wonder.

My parents still to this day act upon their nature to jump onto an idea that excites them, knowing it would be a great decision for the family. This type of go-getting attitude rubbed off on me the older I got. I remember clearly getting ready on my first day, simple attire consisting of black and white, feeling incredibly nervous. I can still remember the smell of the office as I walked up the carpeted stairs, totally petrified of what to expect. I was incredibly thankful to be greeted by a very welcoming middle-aged team, who were patient and passionate about sharing their craft. I was given an in-depth tour of the premise whilst being introduced to members of the team, with an introduction to their specific skillsets. It was clear they understood the need to support the next generation of designers, which meant sharing an open mindset, engaging and encouraging those less skilled, but no less passionate.

My few weeks at AWP Advertising saw me undertake a live project designing a tourism flyer for the City of Chichester, a local town housing one of the most beautiful cathedrals in Sussex. Looking back now, what I thought was a masterpiece was no doubt re-worked by one of the in-house talented designers. However, they let me work on the project from start to finish, they guided me and encouraged me throughout the whole project letting me believe what I had created was worthy of praise. Little did they know they shaped the outlook of my career path and within a few months I was enrolled at college studying Graphic Design with a vision of one day running my own design studio. A few years later upon completion of a Bachelor of Art in Communication Design, I was on the hunt for my first junior position. Unfortunately at this point, where I had undertaken my internship hadn't fared well in the downturn of the local economy and positions outside of London for a country bumpkin, such as myself, were sparse.

I engaged the help of a local job agency to source me interviews, which turned out to be my saviour. One particular role that caught my eye accepted me for interview. The job had a great description however the agency wouldn't disclose the company at the time un-til the company accepted me for interview, something to this day I never understood. However, there I was two days later, walking up to the doors to Carte Blanche Greetings in Chichester, an international greeting card and giftware company.

Now to some this would be amazing, for me not so much... Why? Because I had promised to my older sister that I wouldn't apply for a job there, as she was already an in-house designer. Needless to say, as I was escorted through the design studio housing twenty plus creatives, all eyes were on me because she had alerted the team to my arrival. Talk about feeling like a fish in a bowl.

Yet as I sat in the Art Studio Manager's office, I was all of a sudden made to feel at ease with the realisation of who was sitting across from me. There was Helen, a curly-haired, cheery-voiced character who had been introduced to me years before at AWP Advertising during my internship. Her career had brought her across town to manage the design department at CBG, where she had later employed my sister. At this point I was thankful she recognised me as one of the AWP interns. Out of respect, she asked my sister whether having me as part of the team would cause any upset, yet my sister only encouraged the offer, as she knew the opportunities it would bring me. And so I was employed, my first step on the path to my dream of understanding the world of design.

"I believe fate is choices – it's not chance." - Wayne Newton

The moral is, treat your internship as though it is the stepping stone to your dream job, as one day you may find it was. I credit Helen for believing in me, for nurturing my career and for her leadership

11

ability that built a team I still miss to this day. It was a subliminal turning point in my journey to becoming a better designer. That team makes me strive every day to create the design agency that I am currently continuing to build, based on the encouragement and respect shown to me as a CBG junior. Fifteen years later my journey has found me in Western Australia running my own award-winning design agency, Parklife Group Pty Ltd with my sister as my employee.

"The surest way to make your dreams come true is to live them." - Roy T.Bennett

This book is dedicated to all those who have joined me on my journey, in every position I have held. You have all helped direct my path, but most importantly my family, CBG and Parklife crew, thank you!

Creative
Louise

CEO - Author - Speaker - Mentor
Kate

Sisters

Destined to work together

As a thank you for purchasing this book you have the opportunity to gain access to **facebook.com/groups/etiquetteofanintern**, a closed group for those wanting direct mentorship and advice, as well as access to success stories. Access code: **EOAIsupport**

Your what

"By doing what you love. You inspire & awaken the hearts of others."

– Satuki Shibuya

This was always one of those questions I found incredibly difficult to answer… **What** do you want to be when you grow up? The simple answer from my five-year-old self revolved around Cliff Richards' 'Summer Holiday' movie. I wanted to drive a double decker red bus, whilst singing the ridiculous lyrics to *'We're all going on a summer holiday'*. Looking back now, I think I was onto something! My goal to this day is to one day purchase that London double decker bus, ship it over to Australia and have that pre-fabricated touring design studio that I've recently been ogling in my crazy thoughts.

At sixteen, growing up in a town a fair distance from London, I didn't know what possibilities I had for a career in design. I had times of frustration where I experienced major lows, something I know most young adolescents have. But my dad's career as a car designer found us travelling across continents and being introduced to far afield places growing up, those of much more interest than my hometown. A feeling of 'there's got to be more' had an undercurrent in me to keep pushing forward, which at times being young, had me feeling trapped in a place I knew I wasn't destined to stay.

One thing I established early on was that possibilities only came when I gave myself the chance to find opportunities, by asking for them. I found that by undertaking opportunities it only solidified which direction I wanted to take. In my eyes, no career was black or white. I wanted my craft to continuously grow by undertaking multiple opportunities. Each opportunity I took morphed into a totally different route to what I had initially set out to achieve, yet with each one it helped me to determine my what.

When I started my career in graphic design, never would I ever had thought fifteen years later I would have the knowledge to design and produce products, create their marketing material alongside their digital awareness campaigns, all whilst managing multiple clients and a team. These are skills I picked up through multiple diverse opportunities. The best advice I was ever given by Helen was that as a junior I should 'never stick with any employer for more than two years, if there is no more to be learnt, Keep moving!' This is a hard task when you love your current team but from my experience it is always better to move and return later with more skills than to stick around and turn stale. So just know what you start out with will no doubt in time change, when you allow opportunities in.

Your what

Your why

"If you don't start somewhere, you're gonna go nowhere."

– Bob Marley

Why do you want to undertake an internship? If the answer is to simply make your educator happy, go back to the drawing board. Ask yourself these questions... What do you love doing, what is your passion? **Why** do you want to do it? Gone are the days where you do a job to simply earn a wage, yes that's obviously still important, but with the introduction of digital media, worldwide connectivity, anything is possible by undertaking what you love doing.

Hands down, I love my job. I can't remember the last time I clock watched. The days fly by, which can be a curse when you have a lot of work to complete. But it hasn't always been like this. I have worked for employers who haven't understood a good work culture, which has effected the team's morale. We all will come across times like these in our career journey, but know when it is time to move on, should it not fit in with your personal values. Another opportunity will always be on the horizon. According to statistics we spend about fifty seven per cent of our waking life working during our lifetime. That makes you want to do something you love.

So your homework is to find your what and your why, whilst acknowledging in time it will change. It will morph as you move forward on your journey, but you have to start somewhere.

Why do you want to undertake an internship?

What do you love doing, what is your passion?

Preparation

"Success is where
preparation and
opportunity meet."

– Bobby Unser

These six steps are a guide to how you should prepare to target your selected ideal industry leaders once you determine your what and why. I suggest completing all the below tasks prior to any interaction with possible employers.

To do list

1. Set up a **LinkedIn** account

2. Create a **cover letter**

3. Make a professional looking **resume**

4. Check your **Facebook** account privacy settings

5. Set up a professional **email address** & **email signature**

6. **Google** yourself!

7. Create a professional **voicemail** message

No matter your age, a professional existence on LinkedIn shows you mean business. Take time to fill in all of the necessary information. Be honest and include any work experience or volunteer work you have undertaken.

However, leave areas blank if you have no experience. Honesty goes a long way. Ensure your profile picture is an up-close, professional shot and remember to smile!

Tip: *Set your LinkedIn URL.*

Linked **in**

Linkedin - To do list

(1) Upload a professional image

(2) Write headline

(3) Create summary

(4) Update education history

(5) Add work experience

(6) Add skills

(7) Add volunteer experience

(8) Add accomplishments

(9) Start building your network

Create a Cover Letter

Think of yourself as a product. People don't just buy a product; they buy into the story behind the product. Take time to write a letter that is personalised whilst outlining what you are about, what you want to achieve from the experience and why you have chosen their company to contact.

Tip: *Get three people to spell check it.*

Use business letter format
Place all your contact information and sign your name.

Individualise your cover letter
Each letter you write must be written specifically for each role description.

Provide specific examples
If you say you are great at a particular skillset, give an example.

Emphasise your academic experience
You may have limited work experience so make sure to mention how your strengths and skills have benefited your educational growth.

Include extracurricular experiences
You can also include details about your relevant experience from things such as volunteer work. For example, a history of volunteering in an office-based environment could provide an example of strong interpersonal and organisational skills.

Follow up

Near the end of the letter ensure you mention you will follow up in a week, so they expect your call.

Check your spelling

Did I mention get people to spell check it? Seriously though this in some cases could hurt your chances of getting an internship.

Notes

Make a professional looking Resume

Colour, add some colour! Now in some cases employers' desks can receive multiple applications at any one time, but what is going to make yours stand out? This simple example of a resume outlines the basic elements required.

Ensure to use apps and software that are widely available online to create a resume that stands out above your competition.

Tip: *Get three people to spell check it. This still applies.*

What to include:

1. Contact details

2. Core skills and generic skills

3. Professional headshot

4. Qualifications

5. Character reference(s)

6. Reference contact details

7. Work experience details

COVER LETTER

NAME GOES HERE

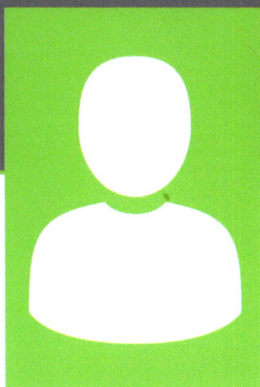

ABOUT THE APPLICANT

Name	Goes here
DOB	Goes here
Mobile	Goes here
Email	Goes here
Address	Goes here

HELLO

Otat. Loratur? Dollest, untet ipsam ea prendes il magnam, nihicimil eaquia dit lam volorib eaquistium dissinciis alignist, qui dolore quae nest id maionse sapelliti occae la et esti volum et facietus aut pos unt optiis ipid eum inciusda etum commossimus doluptati aut que et fugit videm quatque sequi cupti sumquiandio. Ovid quibus alit, ilibus dolut eum dis eatius, offic te et quis pore voluptur sime natem faceptat officillabo. Nem lam eost, voluptatur sitias ratiassimi, quia ad mossimin consectatur, aut ad min consectat liquae natquas ditiuri nonsequam hit ab ilique ea alitint.

Otat. Loratur? Dollest, untet ipsam ea prendes il magnam, nihicimil eaquia dit lam volorib eaquistium dissinciis alignist, qui dolore quae nest id maionse sapelliti occae la et esti volum et facietus aut pos unt optiis ipid eum inciusda etum commossimus doluptati aut que et fugit videm quatque sequi cupti sumquiandio. Ovid quibus alit, ilibus dolut eum dis eatius, offic te et quis pore voluptur sime natem faceptat officillabo. Nem lam eost, voluptatur sitias ratiassimi, quia ad mossimin consectatur, aut ad min consectat liquae natquas ditiuri nonsequam hit ab ilique ea alitint.

Otat. Loratur? Dollest, untet ipsam ea prendes il magnam, nihicimil eaquia dit lam volorib eaquistium dissinciis alignist, qui dolore quae nest id maionse sapelliti occae la et esti volum et facietus aut pos unt optiis ipid eum inciusda etum commossimus doluptati aut que et fugit videm quatque sequi cupti sumquiandio. Ovid quibus alit, ilibus dolut eum dis eatius, offic te et quis pore voluptur sime natem faceptat officillabo. Nem lam eost, voluptatur sitias ratiassimi, quia ad mossimin consectatur, aut ad min consectat liquae natquas ditiuri nonsequam hit ab ilique ea alitint.

SKILLS

- Skill 1
- Skill 2
- Skill 3
- Skill 4

Things to include

- Contact details
- Professional headshot
- Introduction cover letter
- Your four top skills

RESUME

NAME GOES HERE

QUALIFICATIONS

Qualification 1

Qualification 2

Qualification 3

Qualification 4

SKILLS

Skill	★ ★ ★ ★ ★
Skill	★ ★ ★ ★ ★
Skill	★ ★ ★ ★ ★
Skill	★ ★ ★ ★ ★
Skill	★ ★ ★ ★ ★
Skill	★ ★ ★ ★ ★
Skill	★ ★ ★ ★ ★
Skill	★ ★ ★ ★ ★

CHARACTER REFERENCE

Otat. Loratur? Dollest, untet ipsam ea prendes il magnam, nihicimil eaquia dit lam volorib eaquistium dissinciis alignist, qui dolore quae nest id maionse sapelliti occae la et esti.

REFERENCES

Name

Position and Business

Tel Number | Email Address

Name

Position and Business

Tel Number | Email Address

CHARACTER REFERENCE

Otat. Loratur? Dollest, untet ipsam ea prendes il magnam, nihicimil eaquia dit lam volorib eaquistium dissinciis alignist, qui dolore quae nest id maionse sapelliti occae la et esti.

Things to include

- Qualifications
- Character references
- Previous employer references
- Skills

RESUME

WORK EXPERIENCE QUICK GUIDE

in   Please **click here** to see my Linkedin profile

Dates
Position held
Business Name

Dates
Position held
Business Name

Dates
Position held
Business Name

Dates
Position held
Business Name

Dates
Position held
Business Name

Dates
Position held
Business Name

IT SKILLS

Word 5/6   Excel 5/6   Indesign 6/6   Illustrator 6/6   Photoshop 6/6

Things to include

• Linkedin URL link
• Employment history
• Work experience/placement history
• IT skill levels

Check your Facebook account

All employers will Facebook stalk possible interns. If they say they don't they are either bending the truth or they aren't active on Facebook. With this in mind, ensure your accessible content is either tame or your security is on allowing only restricted access. The most important part… Your pictures!

Ensure your cover and profile pictures paint you in your best light. No matter your security settings, these images will always be accessible.

Tip: *Delete any questionable images.*

Notes

Set up a professional email address & email signature

yourname@gmail.com, boring right? Yes, but does it paint a better picture than loudmouthrazzle@gmail.com. We shouldn't judge, but we do. How you are digitally perceived can give a distorted picture of you and lead to missed opportunities.

Tip: *Set up a professional email address alongside an email signature that shows you are prepared and professional.*

Email Signature Necessities;

• Your Name
• Your Telephone Number
• Your LinkedIn URL

Email signatures need only be simple yet can ensure you portray an organised and professional presence.

	Your Name	
	Mob	0000 000 000
	Tel	0000 000 000
	Skype	skypename
	Linkedin	www.linkedin.com/in/namegoeshere

Google yourself

It's always worth Googling yourself to ensure any unwanted info is either removed or at least managed. Being prepared is the best way to enter an interview.

To do list

○
○
○
○
○
○
○
○
○
○
○

Notes

Research your ideal employer

"You will never get a
second chance to make
a first impression."

– Will Rogers

Prior to even thinking of getting in touch with your list of prospective companies, research them in detail via their website, social media, as well as employees in common.

- What is the company's mission, vision and values?
- Do they align with yours?
- Does it sound like a culture that you will fit alongside?
- Who are the company decision makers? Connect with them on LinkedIn!
- What is the company's culture like?

This may sound simple but it's surprising how much you can find out when you allow the time to absorb relevant information. It also allows you to bypass HR when you discover just who those decision makers are. Why be added to a pile when you can connect directly on LinkedIn and go straight to the top? Connect and once accepted, politely email acknowledging their company, what it stands for and how you feel you would benefit from undertaking an internship under their watchful eye.

"Research is what I'm doing when I don't know what I'm doing." – Wernher Von Braun

Ideal Employer 1

Ideal Employer 2

Ideal Employer 3

Ideal Employer 4

Ideal Employer 5

Ideal Employer 6

How to deliver your resume

"The best way to predict the future is to create it."

– Abraham Lincoln

How many emails do you think the average CEO receives per day? A LOT! For this reason it is always a great idea to hand deliver a well-presented resume by hand. If you aren't able to make it past reception, make sure the receptionist knows you want your resume to go directly to the decision maker. Before you leave, find out this person's name and email address. Email them immediately to alert them your resume has been left with reception and you would appreciate them taking a look to see if your strengths would suit an internship with the company. Ensure your resume is printed on good quality paper, your cover letter is well thought out and you deliver it presented in a folder that makes it stand out from your possible competitors. Treat it as if you are applying for a job, its not 'just' an internship, its an opportunity!

I have had cases of parents calling me to request their son/daughter undertake an internship with us. Understandably some potential young interns are shy, but you must try and take responsibility for ensuring your own career path by pushing yourself to make direct contact. You may be incredibly shy but carry yourself with confidence. Although you may be screaming on the inside with fear, externally you can portray yourself to be a confident young professional. So please ensure all correspondence is done directly.

Resilience is the ability to "bounce back" from stressful or challenging experiences. It involves being able to adapt to changes and approach negative events, sources of stress and traumatic events as constructively as possible.

How to present yourself

"Always present yourself as a person who expects to succeed."

– Barbara Bradford

How you dress represents your character, but know we must adapt to our surroundings when it comes to the corporate world. Make sure you dress accordingly and show up fifteen minutes early to your interview.

Prior to starting an internship, make sure to touch base with your supervisor to ask any questions relating to dress policy. The knack is to slip in confidently alongside your peers whilst ensuring a professional image. It really does depend on the industry you enter, but make sure as well as 'fitting in' that you feel comfortable.

Tips: *Dress to impress even when you deliver your resume. Don't show up wearing hoodies or short skirts should you be entering the corporate world to deliver your resume!! Remember you are on 'show' even before you get to reception. You don't know who you might be sharin the lift with you!*

If you are feeling under the weather, it's time to bring out your best confidence boosting outfit to make everyone think you're feeling fine.
If you choose to still go in, make sure to always maintain a professional image no matter what.

Notes

Notes

You've received a placement offer

"Have an attitude of gratitude."

– Thomas S. Monson

Congratulations!

When you get this fantastic news, make sure to formally accept their offer via email or post, thanking them for the opportunity. Also take this opportunity to request they send you any company information that will support your internship prior to commencing.

Tip: *Take time to research the company across its social media platforms so you walk in on that first day with a knowledge base.*

Research

Your first week

"By doing what you love. You inspire & awaken the hearts of others."

– Satuki Shibuya

Although this mentions the first week, ensure you practice these simple tasks throughout your internship…

1. Always show up ten minutes early

2. Say hello and goodbye to all those present in the office whilst ensuring to give eye contact and shake hands!

3. On occasion, bring baked goods to share between the team. This shows a friendly, collaborative mindset towards the business and its team members.

4. Ask Questions, what internal communication platforms do they use? Can you gain access?

5. At the end of each day, email or present a summary of work undertaken to your supervisor.

6. Use your initiative; try to figure out a problem prior to asking for help.

Questions to ask

1. Who is your supervisor?
    (If it hasn't already been made clear.)

2. What are your responsibilities?

3. When can you take a lunch break and for how long?

4. Do you need to sign in and out?

5. If for unforeseen reasons you are sick or going to be late what is the best number to call?

Tip: *Store this to your phone straight away!*

Remembering names

This is a great technique I learnt whilst networking, I am absolutely useless at learning names, I have never been able to retain them. However, I was recently advised of this tip:

Repeat their name back to them when introductions occur.

So if Lisa introduces herself as Lisa, say *"Hello 'Lisa' it's great to meet you"*. This repetition allows your brain to store the information easier. A simple hack that we at our design studio totally stand behind!

Be time wise

People tend to underestimate how long a task should take, so when you're working out the timeline of a project, be generous in your estimates.

Tip: *Don't take on more than you can handle.*

Keep a journal

"Acquiring the habit of note taking is a wonderfully complementary skill to that of listening."

– Richard Branson

Make sure to take time to write about your activities, feelings and insights, as it will become an important part of your internship. It provides an opportunity to record your discussions with your supervisor and team members, as well as observations about your experience. It challenges you to critically think about your work, allowing an excellent way to improve and document your internship experience. Rereading it can later provide insights and understandings that can serve as a foundation for your final report.

How to keep a journal

Set aside a regular scheduled time to write in your journal. It won't work unless you update it often. Playing catch up will have you inserting information that is not fresh in your mind, allowing for missed information.

There are several ways to keep a good journal.

Informal journal keeping

1. If you feel that you have a lot to say, then simply write.

2. Reflect on topics that concern you, and which will help you to clarify your goals.

One useful technique to keep yourself actively involved in your experience is to write and respond to questions.

"If you are not willing to risk the usual, you will have to settle for the ordinary." – Jim Rohn

Listed below are some questions that may help you in this process.

1. What was the most important thing I learnt today?
2. What did I observe about how the company's philosophy affects the way people do their jobs?
3. What did I do when I needed help?
4. What facts or terms do I want to remember?
5. What moral and ethical questions did I face or ignore?
6. What human relations problems occurred? Could I have done anything to improve them?
7. Did I hear any opinions or interpretations that differ from my own?
8. How would I change this day if I tried it again tomorrow?

Example

Q1

Write your question here

Write your answer here

Journal Entry 1

Date

Q1

Q2

Q3

Q4

Journal Entry 2

Date

Q1

Q2

Q3

Q4

Journal Entry 3

Date

Q1

Q2

Q3

Q4

Journal Entry 4

Date

Q1

Q2

Q3

Q4

Journal Entry 5

Date

Q1

Q2

Q3

Q4

Journal Entry 6

Date

Q1

Q2

Q3

Q4

Journal Entry 7

Date

Q1

Q2

Q3

Q4

Journal Entry 8

Date

Q1

Q2

Q3

Q4

Journal Entry 9

Q1

Q2

Q3

Q4

Journal Entry 10

Date

Q1

Q2

Q3

Q4

Journal Entry 11

Date

Q1

Q2

Q3

Q4

Journal Entry 12

Date

Q1

Q2

Q3

Q4

Journal Entry 13

Date

Q1

Q2

Q3

Q4

Journal Entry 14

Date

Q1

Q2

Q3

Q4

Journal Entry 15

Date

Keep a journal

Q1

Q2

Q3

Q4

Journal Entry 16

Date

Q1

Q2

Q3

Q4

Journal Entry 17

Date

Q1

Q2

Q3

Q4

Journal Entry 18

Date

Q1

Q2

Q3

Q4

Journal Entry 19

Keep a journal

Q1

Q2

Q3

Q4

The BIG No Nos

"Knowledge will give you power, but character respect."

– Bruce Lee

Mobile phones... Put them away!

- Let your friends and family know of your new position and that you will not be available via mobile during your agreed working hours.

- Ensure you make an effort to leave your mobile stored away when you aren't on your lunch break.

These small gestures show you respect your position and you are focused on the task at hand. It's a huge disappointment for supervisors when they see interns sitting using their phones and not giving the internship program their full attention.

It's 'not just' a breezy internship!

Treat this opportunity as a three-month employment probation, as in the eyes of your intern supervisor, that's exactly what it is. You are there to prove you were made for their team and that after your internship you are too valuable for them to let you go.

Whether you are looking for employment or a network prior to starting your higher education, it can make for an opportunity of a lifetime.

Feedback

You may not be used to receiving feedback from a busy and stressed supervisor, who may deliver feedback in a less than ideal way. Don't take it personally and get defensive. If a situation is worth discussing further, ensure to schedule a time with your supervisor to discuss in depth. Understand that the best lessons come from the toughest teachers!

Demeaning tasks

No task is beneath you, try not to get precious if asked to do what may be considered a demeaning task. Smile and do as requested graciously and do it well.

Ignoring instructions or advice

When you are offered instruction or constructive criticism, take it on board and action it. Know that those offering it already have industry experience. If you don't necessarily agree with it, ensure to ask in a respectful way why an alternative method would be more suited. By asking, you are simply clarifying as well as being inquisitive. Your supervisor should welcome this, as you are undertaking the internship to learn tricks of the trade and alternative methods. So remember the next time you receive constructive criticism from your supervisor, use this simple process to handle it with respect and professionalism:

1. Stop your first reaction

2. Remember the positives of receiving feedback

3. Listen to ensure understanding

4. Say thank you

5. Deconstruct the feedback by asking questions

6. Request a time to follow up

In sickness and in health

"Trust the process."

– Gary Zukav

There will come times during an internship where either the intern or business need to reschedule due to sickness or holiday. Below are some guides to ensure you portray a professional commitment to your role.

Above any form of communication, make sure to call your supervisor directly to alert them of your absence. If you are unable to get through to your supervisor, make sure to follow up with an email explaining your absence.

Tip: *Do not text your supervisor. If you were employed you would be required to call, so make sure to follow similar protocols to that of an employed role.*

Make sure to make note of any absent days and to schedule alternative days to replace lost time.

Absent Date

Replacement Date

Upon completion

"There is nothing more
rewarding than
completing a goal you have
set for yourself."

– Jerry Seinfeld

Landing your dream internship is only the first step to understanding whether the career path you had in mind is the right one. Come the end of your internship, it's especially important to keep up your momentum and finish strong.

Here's how to leave a lasting impression on your supervisor and make the most of your internship before it ends.

Ask for feedback

Your supervisor isn't just a whiz at his/her position but also a big help when it comes to your development as a student and an up-and-coming member of the workplace. Show that you're open to constructive criticism by requesting feedback before your internship is over.

Long-term planning

Try to think ahead about how you want this internship to fit into your career trajectory: Would you like to return? Have you had enough? If you are interested in sticking with the company long-term, express that politely to your supervisor. Your internship will have lasting value no matter what you choose, but it's up to you to later turn it into a job.

List your accomplishments and update your resume

Record all of your hard work whilst it is still relevant and fresh in your mind. Update your resume as a top priority.

Build your portfolio

Your resume summarises your achievements, but it doesn't provide any tangible evidence of your work. Following your supervisor's written permission, keep copies of your finished projects. An effective compilation can include anything from creative projects and published articles to presentations, depending on your field.

Get a letter of recommendation

Ask for the letter to be a general recommendation based on your performance, rather than a letter tailored specifically for a future job or internship, and be sure to get the okay from your supervisor to potentially use it for multiple future applications.

Follow up and say "thank you."

Small gestures will get you noticed, something as simple as a hand-written note can go a long way. Ensure to write to each member of the team that were a direct influence and support throughout the internship. You can be less personal with other members of staff and send them an email thanking them.

To do list

○

○

○

○

○

○

○

○

○

○

○

○

○

○

Let's start the journey

Bonus Book

The Intern Employers' Guide

STEPS TO SECURE AND ENSURE A MOTIVATED INTERN

A tool for ambitious business owners

The Intern Employers' Guide

Written by Kate Stagg, CEO | Parklife Group Pty Ltd™

Introduction

"Our aspirations are
our possibilities."

– Samuel Johnson

The book you are holding was inspired by a desire to encourage youth to be driven and motivated in their quest for career success. It is designed to act as a support tool, to help guide and nurture an intern through the daunting journey of entering the workforce.

I knew when I began writing that I wanted to create a book for both the intern and the employer to help support the entire process from start to finish. I chose to merge the workbook and guide, so both the intern and employer would understand expectations. Whether you have already undertaken interns in your workplace or whether you are thinking about introducing an internship program into your business, take time to read both sides of this book.

The intern workbook, *Etiquette of an Intern*, is the perfect gift for a potential intern looking to enter the workforce.

Your why

"We rise by lifting others."

– Robert Ingersoll

Why are you thinking of taking on an intern? You may want to support youth looking to establish work experience, to help them get that 'foot on the ladder'. Maybe you are looking to mentor the next up and coming generation of workers in your industry, or simply supporting your local educational facilities by offering their students an amazing experience.

Here are five benefits of undertaking an internship program:

A new perspective

Interns challenge the status quo and bring new ways to undertake new ideas to the company. Interns are good at questioning processes and can often see a better way of doing things that a manager might not.

Technology savvy

Social media, computer programs, iPads, these are a piece of cake for young professionals. And although you may be a young entrepreneur, you can always use a hand from a fellow Gen Y tech-savvy professional.

Trial talent

An internship is a great way to see how much potential a student or recent graduate has in the field. You'll get to see their skills and work ethic as an intern. This could turn into a paid position later.

Tackle time-short tasks

Interns are great to help tackle those projects that we as business owners are too time poor to undertake. This is a great opportunity to hand over live projects, allowing for meaningful work to be completed that will help your business run smoother, accomplish more, or be more successful.

Gain brand advocates

Hiring an intern helps spread the word about your company, whether you mean to or not. If you're an impressive internship supervisor and mentor, your interns will probably talk about their experience with peers, friends and family members, essentially advertising your business.

If you do want to bring on interns, consider what goals you'd like them to reach by the end of the internship.

However, don't hire an intern for any of these reasons below:

Free labour

Undertaking an internship program isn't something to take on lightly, you need to ensure you can provide mentorship and training to the intern in order for them to build on their skillset throughout their placement. An intern shouldn't be taken on simply in place of a paid employee to save on costs.

You're too busy

If you know you don't have time to be a good supervisor, you don't have time for an intern. You need to enable accessibility and a constant feed of mentorship and training. Otherwise it won't turn out to be beneficial for either party.

You don't have a clear program

Just because you need additional help does not mean you should hire interns. Instead, you can consider hiring temporary employees or contractors to help with your workload.

Creating an internship program

"Tell me and I forget, teach me and I may remember, involve me and I learn."

– Benjamin Franklin

The question remains: What can interns, first-time employees and business owners do to make sure the experience is beneficial for all involved?

Here are four strategies that will help guide you:

State your expectations up front

The first few days on the job aren't just about orientation and filling out paperwork, but setting the tone. As supervisor, you should talk about what they hope to gain from the experience at your company. Anticipate questions to save yourself time. Write out procedures for the little things you take for granted, such as using your phone system. One way to do this is to create a cloud-based training video guide that interns can reference any time they have a question.

Tip: *Have ongoing projects that interns can work on when they finish specific assignments.*

Establish an open-door policy

Your intern is there to learn from you. Everyone is busy and it's so easy to get caught up, so schedule weekly appointments into your diary to ensure time is set aside to see how everything is going in addition to the day-to-day projects and tasks.

Help them help you

Interns can learn a lot about the position and how it's changed and grown from the people who sat at their desk before them, so schedule some time for the old and new to share their ideas, skills and experience.

Review your needs

Remember, an intern will be looking for good experience, so be sure your needs match those of the interns. Ask yourself the following questions:

- How can an intern help you with your business goals?
- Do you have enough work to support an intern?
  Think about short-term and long-term assignments.
- Who will supervise and mentor your intern?
- What ongoing training can you provide?
- Do you have available office space and other resources?

Create

Today's leap forward
is tomorrow's dream
come true

Adele Basheer

Is your business ready?

"Don't watch the clock; do what it does. Keep going."

– Sam Levenson

The questions below are designed to help you determine if your company is prepared to manage an internship program, how your business can benefit from having an intern, and how a student-intern would benefit from working with you. These questions do not require a formal response; however, I recommended that you think about the answers.

You may also find that the answers provide a foundation for creating the internship position description.

- How do you see your company benefiting from hosting an intern? Would your business benefit from the work of interns to write, research, identify leads, work with clients, or provide overall organisation or program support?

- What are the goals of your business's internship program? Do you need assistance completing a particular project? Do you hope to use the program as a pipeline for potential full-time employees? Do you seek to cultivate talent in young professionals?

- What do you want the intern to learn while interning at your organisation?

- Would having interns benefit current staff members by providing managerial and supervisory experience?

- What type of project work needs to be completed?

- Is there an individual in the company who will serve as the intern's supervisor and point of contact for a university?

- Do you have the support of senior management?

- Does your company have the space and resources to support an intern and his/her duties?

- What is the intended duration of the internship? Will the need to fill this position be ongoing, or complete after one term?

- What time of year can you host an intern? What are ideal start and end dates for the internship? Is this a part-time or full-time internship?

- Are specific skills or technical knowledge/experience required to adequately complete the assigned tasks?

- Are you looking for an intern in a particular program of study?

- Can your company offer opportunities for unique industry experiences during the internship?

- Is this a paid or unpaid internship?

- Are you able to develop and implement a training and orientation program for new interns?

Notes

Four reasons why your business needs interns

"The energy of the mind is the essence of life."

– Aristotle

I have used interns effectively throughout my career, in both my own company and previous businesses I have contracted for. They have made a significant difference in the growth of each company. I've outlined four key advantages to hiring interns that you might consider if you're looking to build your business.

They come with a lot of energy

Given the opportunity, interns come eager to learn and full of life. Due to most internships only being a part-time arrangement it also enables them to come refreshed and energised ready to get stuck in. However, they do need some light management and guidance to make sure their energy is pointed in the right direction. Make sure to provide clear objectives, suggestions for achieving those objectives and then meet once a week to refine their activities to achieve those objectives.

They are inexpensive

Since there are not a lot of overhead costs associated with hiring interns, the overall burdens and risks of using them are very low. The most expensive cost is the time you give them. What is your time worth?

They come with fresh ideas

It is really true that young people have good ideas, in part because they come to problems from a position of naiveté, which is actually an asset.

It really is true good interns turn out to be some of the best full-time employees

Again, this point may be obvious but it is important. Internships are not just a way of attracting full-time candidates; they're a way of finding and hiring new full-time employees who are familiar with your corporate culture.

Writing the internship position description

"If you havent found it yet, keep looking."

– Steve Jobs

What Do You Need to Include?

Treat an intern job description as you would if you were on the lookout for a full-time employee. It is important to create a detailed yet clear description that outlines responsibilities and qualifications for the position.

In order to attract applicants that fit the needs of the intern position, ensure you list the basic requirements. A list of these can be found below.

Items to Include in the Internship Position Description:

- The name of your organization
- Location
- A contact person to whom application/resumes will be sent
- The contact's phone number and email address
- The internship position title
- Description of responsibilities and tasks
- Qualifications or required skills
- Information about scheduling/hours
- Desired start date and/or anticipated end date
- Duration
- Compensation and/or wages
- What do you want applicants to supply when applying?
- Training offered
- Expected learning outcomes

Intern tasks

"Before you start anything,
learn how to finish it."

– Teddy Roosevelt

Does your company have a list of 'to dos' that you would like to undertake yet just don't have the time to complete them? Maybe a specific department is in need of additional support. Taking on an intern can be a great solution to support the needs of the business while providing hands on experience to an intern.

In addition to the specific projects planned for the intern, the following list illustrates other tasks commonly carried out by interns.

These lists may be useful when creating the position description and when assigning duties throughout the internship.

Accounting/Business/Finance

- Create documents/spread sheets
- Attend client and staff meetings
- Review financial information
- Provide customer service
- Participate in training sessions
- Analyse data to identify areas of opportunity and efficiency
- Generate financial forecast and cost recovery reports

Arts/Design

- Create artwork and designs
- Schedule/attend client meetings; communicate with clients about their designs
- Proofread communications
- Work on a specific project or multiple projects
- Create portfolio of projects
- Design email templates, logos, graphics for emails and blogs, HTML build-out, Web banners, website

Education

- Create and implement lesson plans
- Decorate/organize classroom
- Assist students with projects
- Attend and participate in teacher/staff meetings
- Monitor student progress

Fashion

- Draft original designs and create patterns
- Communicate with clients
- Support trade shows, retail events and fashion shows
- Perform quality control
- Conduct market research and brand outreach
- Engage in fabric lays, sewing and production

Government

- Attend committee meetings
- Prepare meeting minutes
- Maintain blogs/social media
- Create or modify documents and memos
- Work with lobbyists
- Assist with research projects
- Research legislative and regulatory issues

Human Resources

- File applications from prospective candidates, process applications, and purge outdated applications
- Schedule interviews; generate letters/emails confirming receipt of applications from job candidates
- Plan, arrange space for, and execute classes and meetings
- Check candidate licensures and verify professional references
- Prepare materials for workshops or new hire orientations

Information Technology

- Update and install hardware and software
- Take Help Desk calls and provide customer service to callers
- Create and maintain spread sheets, databases and reports
- Perform equipment maintenance
- Maintain social media or company website

Marketing/Advertising/Public Relations

- Create, edit and implement marketing plans
- Create newsletters and client communications
- Maintain blog, social media and websites
- Prepare press releases
- Research potential new clients
- Schedule and/or attend client meetings
- Support trade show and third-party partner initiatives

Non-Profit/Human Services

- Engage in fundraising and donor activities
- Coordinate volunteer activities
- Prepare news releases and communications
- Support staff in program development and implementation; transcribe case notes
- Observe or provide direct care to clients in programs to ensure their well-being

Paralegal/Law

- Review and approve proposed contracts; act as a liaison with external lawyers and technical personnel
- Analyse and identify legal issues in cases
- Research methods of acquiring further evidence including affidavit or interrogatories, further hearings, etc./ conduct legal research
- Communicate with clients; attend staff/client meetings
- Organize files/notes
- Draft/ prepare legal documents

Videography/Production

- Develop and produce storyboards and videos
- Produce clips and B-roll for press, presenters, website, etc.
- Watermark video of full pieces, copy/create repertoire DVDs
- Update/maintain video database
- Assist with post-production activities
- Schedule/attend video/photography shoots

General Duties

- Collect, record, analyse or verify data and information from various sources
- Set up client files; data entry of client information and case notes
- Use software to compile and generate reports, statistics, time-lines, tables, graphs, correspondence or presentations
- Communicate with clients
- Draft newsletters and correspondence
- Maintain social media sites
- Organize/create spread sheets
- Write handbooks or manuals
- Design posters, graphs or charts
- Develop presentations
- Conduct research
- Observe professionals in their industry
- Attend and/or participate in professional meetings and presentations

Choosing an intern

"Choose people who choose you."

– Michelle Obama

The first step to choosing an intern is taking the time to analyse their resume

- What are their strengths and weaknesses?
- What skills can they bring to the team?
- Did their cover letter resonate with you?
- Do their skills align with your internship program?

Tip: *Undertake a background check across their social media platforms.*

Hiring interns can be a challenge. Although candidates may look good on paper, interviews often reveal a whole different story. Next step is inviting the selected few for an interview.

Here are some things to look for in the interview:

- Did they arrive early?
- Was the applicant a good listener?
- Did the applicant have good communication skills?
- Demonstrated Interpersonal/teamwork abilities?
- Did they offer flexibility?

Tip: *Offer the two top candidates a one-day trial to undertake administrative tasks to assess who is best suited to your program. It's a great way to see if they fit in with your team.*

New start procedures

"The secret of getting ahead is getting started."

– Mark Twain

The best advice I can give you is to schedule an orientation at the start, to enable you to run through everything in full with the intern. Ensure you talk through the following points so everything is transparent, whilst stating your expectations in full.

cation supervisor.seg

Insurance

Ensure your insurance covers the internship program or that the intern provides specific insurance documentation from their education supervisor.

Job description

Take time to go through the job description in detail in order for the intern to fully understand their role and expectations. This is a great time to discuss your expectations and answer any questions the intern may have. Literally lay it all out on the table.

Tour

During the tour of your premise ensure you point out all fire exits, as well as fire extinguishers and where the first aid box is located. Make sure to introduce the intern to your First Aid Supervisor(s).

Location

Locate the intern's desk and introduce the intern to all employees within close proximity and allow them time to settle in. Make it a responsibility of one of the neighbouring employees to introduce them to staff throughout the building, which will help forge friendships between employees.

Briefing

Once the intern has settled in, take time to go through the program briefing in detail alongside providing them login access to the internal communication system whether it be email or another system you have in place.

Non disclosure and IP agreement

If you haven't already done so, make sure this is signed to protect your own company and that of your clients.

Document each intern's journey

"Record-keeping is important. Document everything you you do."

– Frank Degen

The most important advice you should take on board, is to document every step of an interns journey to ensure all communication is saved for any unforeseen situation such as a complaint.

All communication done by email is great as it will be stored, but any communication undertaken verbally should be documented such as:

Meetings

Take note of all discussions from meetings, alongside tasks, to action as an outcome of the meeting.

Tasks

Clearly layout weekly tasks in a clear manner for interns. Maintain a hard copy of each week's task sheet.

Review

Upon completion of the intern's review, make sure to create a report based on what was discussed. This review is then to be gone through with the intern for them to agree on the contained information.

We
rise
by
lifting
others

www.ingramcontent.com/pod-product-compliance
Lightning Source LLC
Chambersburg PA
CBHW041306210326
41598CB00011B/858